BECOMING UNMASKED

Exposing the Real You

UNETTA LOFTON

Scripture references are used with permission from Zondervan via Biblegateway.com

ISBN 978-1-950861-56-9

PRINTED IN THE UNTIED STATES OF AMERICA

His Glory Creations Publishing, LLC
Wendell, North Carolina

HIS GLORY

DEDICATION

I would like to dedicate this book to my brother and sister, Antwan and Vernecia Lofton. You two are my heart. Although our mom is gone, I also dedicate this to my late mom, Pastor Shelley Lofton. She taught me how to live a Godly life. I dedicate this book to anyone who feels like they can't make it, to anyone who is struggling to understand where you fit in life.

ACKNOWLEDGMENTS

First, I thank God for blessing me with this opportunity. I give a big thank you to Minister Diane Pace for the push and support to start this journey on writing. Even though I had told her, I was not a writer, she was persistent.

I would also like to acknowledge those who have encouraged me to follow God and follow through.

I especially would like to thank my publisher, Minister Felicia Lucas and her extraordinary staff.

Also, I want to acknowledge CEO Pastor Anna Lyons and the Women of Triumph Ministries International Inc.; thank you to my leaders Pastor Larry Stancil and Apostle Dr. Hattie Stancil as well as my church family, Harvest Word Ministries in Zebulon, N.C.

TABLE OF CONTENTS

FOREWORD

I have known Unetta all her natural life. Our families were neighbors and we lived within walking distance of each other. Although we were neighbors, we did not visit each other's homes. We were raised in church. We were known as the "Holy Ghost" kids because we were always in church services. Unetta's great uncle was a pillar in the community. He was my Pastor. Unetta's family would attend there when they were not at their church. Growing up, our mothers required us to attend church. Unlike this generation, our parents did not give us an option to lay-out of church. In our homes, holiness was a lifestyle. That is pretty much all we knew…church, church, church. Unetta grew up as a preacher's kid. Her mother was a very private individual. They never had other kids over to visit. In the book, Unetta explains how life was much more different in the United States Army. There was so much freedom and so many choices to make. Although there were many choices, she still chose to do what was spiritually and morally right.

This book will help you understand the importance of knowing your purpose. I look at Unetta now, and I think of how none of the church-going and teachings has been in vain. She has found her purpose. I can see the spiritual teachings that were poured into her bursting forth. From the little kid being drug off to church to the powerfully anointed woman of God she is today. All that churching has paid off. I have always admired Unetta for being the anointed vocalist that many people know her to be.

As an adult, I can remember her coming to visit her great uncle's church from time to time, and my daughter Renee and I would hunch each other and say, "There's Unetta. Maybe she's going to sing." We always looked forward to hearing Unetta sing. As I fast forward to the present, I must say, Unetta has been utilizing her teachings. This book will enlighten you on who this shy, comical, powerfully anointed, angelic singing, country girl with the million dollars smile truly is and where she comes from. You will learn who poured into her and how she continues to walk in and add to those standards. She is a very joyful person to be in the presence of. Through the years, she has learned how to balance her walk as a Christian. Her background as a preacher's kid comes forth in her daily walk. Unetta is single and she does not have any children. She spends most of her time doing Kingdom Work. She loves to study the Gospel, sing, travel, read, and support others.

In the book, you will see Unetta is continually active on this Christian journey. Midway through the introduction, she says, "Often times I had to be delivered from me." Wow! Accepting the need to be delivered from ourselves can be a tough pill to swallow. Unetta openly explained some of the rejection and challenges she overcame. The chapters in this journey of her life teaches life's lessons and challenges of how if Jesus has to reach way down, He can pick you up. It encourages you to know that only God can validate you. Unetta expresses the outcome of being delivered from self and allowing the Holy Spirit to direct you. It will inspire you to search inside of yourself to find your purpose, to know that you are wonderfully and fearfully made, and to live the life God intended. Once you unmask and are delivered from YOU, then you will realize that only God can validate you. Congratulations on your first of many solos!

Diane Pace, CEO and Founder of Walking Worthy
Visionary Entrepreneur, Inspirational Speaker, Author
walkingworthyisa.weebly.com

INTRODUCTION

Do you sometimes ask yourself, where is my life taking me? What is my purpose here? This may include you looking closely at yourself. As I journey on this road, I've had to stop and look at me. Yes, being saved wasn't enough. I felt there had to be more. Often, I had to be delivered from me. Examining myself was a start for me to grow in my Christian walk. As I open some of myself in this book, I will share my walk and challenges in church and personal life. Boy, did I have to lay aside every weight! I had to surrender all. As you read my book, my prayer is that it helps you overcome every challenge in your life and become the best you in this Christian walk. My goal is to inspire and encourage as many as possible through this book.

CHAPTER 1

SPARE THE ROD, SPOIL THE CHILD

I am a Southern girl and proud of it, lol. As stated, I was born in Smithfield, NC, at Johnston Memorial Hospital. I was raised in Middlesex NC, as they say, down South, where there is plenty of farmland. I have two wonderful siblings. My growing up was unique. I grew up around or raised by many prominent Christian examples and environment.

My uncle, aunt, grandma, and mom were all either Pastors or just holiness bible-believing people. Growing up, when you heard the phrase 'my parents drug us to church,' well, that was very true in my childhood. I was not really a people person. I was an observer and, most of the time, stayed to myself. I did not have a lot of friends. I didn't socialize a lot. I didn't have a best friend while growing up, at least not until I went to Elementary school. I was a little mischievous.

My mother, the late Pastor Shelley Lofton, brought me up in church. My background is holiness. So yes, I was called a holy roller. Of course, my mom and others had to explain the speaking in tongues. My church home was Selma Church of God of Prophecy. It was normal on a Sunday to get up hearing "Jesus is love" by The Commodores. I can remember mom pressing our hair on Sunday mornings. Growing up, I sang with the Victory Ensemble at Selma and my mom was one of the choir directors. We had night services at 7:30 pm.

Until I was of age, my mom would drop me off at my great grandma's house, Juanita Stancil (which everyone called ma Nita). Everyone loved this woman. I would play and help grandma clean the house till ma got back from work. I didn't do sleepovers; my mom didn't play that. She was very strict. I would occasionally visit my uncle Pastor Sylvester Holder's church which is St. James Holiness church in Middlesex, NC. I pretty much went to service with great-grandma Juanita, Grandma Ethel King, and of course, my mom. Although I wasn't a people person, I think my smile attracted many people.

My fondest memory is great-grandma Juanita Stancil would attend this church, Stancil Chapel, with that Pastor being Pastor Julia Watson. Someone had bought me a little red drum set. Whenever I would go with my great grandma to church, they would ask us to sing, and I would beat my little drum. I would also take it over to my uncle's church sometimes, I would sing there as well. I liked that cause at that time, I enjoyed the attention we were getting.

One of the fond memories was that I loved to go to St. James and see my Aunt Ruby sitting in the corner beating her tambourine with her big stylish hat. Another great memory I love today is a service my Uncle Sylvester had started called People-to-People Day. Uncle Sylvester had started People-to-People Day so people could learn and meet the dignitaries in Johnston County. Every year in October, Uncle Sylvester would invite a lot of politicians, law enforcement, the ROTC cadets from High School, Seymore Johnson Air Force to do a fly over. Man, it would be packed!

The best part was my grandma and some of the saints from the church would have this spread afterwards. Boy, was that some good food! Looking back over my life, I credit two people who played a major part in my upbringing, and that's my great-grandma and my mother. The bible speaks in Proverbs of a virtuous woman. I was blessed to have two in my life. My great-grandma Juanita Stancil was kind, humble, soft-spoken, and so well spoken of and highly respected by those in the community they called her Ma Nita. Her house was like a Hospice for those who grew ill. She taught me humility and to always pray and be humble in whatever I do. My mom, oh my! She taught me strength, courage, faith, commitment, and perseverance.

As I stated before, my mom raised me as a single parent, with the help of close family members and a couple of her close friends, and you know who you are, lol. Through her sickness, she pressed to work every day, continued her duties at the church faithfully (and she held almost every position in the church till she became Pastor). Even through struggles and pain, she showed strength and character. She smiled, believing in Faith that everything would work out. She truly showed that mustard seed faith. Luke 17:6 "If you have faith the size of a mustard seed, you can say to this mulberry tree, 'Be uprooted and planted in the sea,' and it will obey you. Needless to say, she did an outstanding job raising me. I admired these two women and credited them for my upbringing. I think I took the most whoopings, lol. My mom truly believed in Proverbs 13:24, spare the rod and spoil the child. I was well disciplined. My childhood was very simple, surrounded by much love.

CHAPTER 2

TRAIN UP A CHILD IN THE WAY HE SHOULD GO

As I began this journey, I always had Proverbs 22:6 in mind. Train up a child in the way he should go, and when he is old, he will not depart from it. I started in head start and went on up to elementary school at Glendale-Kenly Elementary in Micro-Kenly, NC. I have never been a school fan, but I took a great stab at it. I took basic courses that didn't require much brain power, lol. I kept good grades. The culture at school was mixed with black and white kids. I didn't have to pay for my lunch, which was great. My mom would drop us off at my great grandma's house to catch the bus before she went to work.

I was fortunate to gain a good friend while being in elementary school. Our friendship was all the way through to high school. We really hit it off, and she didn't care that I was a preacher's kid. She was very nice, and she also had my back while we were in school. When someone picked on me or made fun of me because of being a preacher's kid, she would put them in their place. I didn't have to say a word. The school I went to was in good condition for the most part. I did not engage in any sports. I wasn't athletic inclined. I just loved to watch. I spent most of my after-school evenings doing homework or going to a band service or revival.

In church, we had Band service, which was made up of a small group of people. Usually, around seven to eight people would go into someone's home and have a little mini service which lasted about an hour. My mom oversaw the band, so of course, I had to go. Or if there was a revival and if mom had to preach or someone from the church, I went to support. Every now and then, she would leave me with our grandmas, but that was not much. Where she went, I went. I guess being a PK (Preacher's Kid), sometimes people think you're a pushover or you're just supposed to take things. So yes, I was challenged, especially this one time.

This one girl on the school bus kept running off at the mouth. I kept telling her to leave me alone, but she kept at it. So, I was at the point I had it, I stood up, she pushed me, and I wailed on her so hard even she was shocked. So, her response after the fact was, "You are supposed to be preacher's kid." I responded back, "No, my mom is saved, I am not, so don't get it twisted." I think everyone got the message.

Growing up, I did not know what I wanted to be until later in life. At that time, I think I was always trying to fit in or find my identity through my life. On the spiritual side, I wanted to be a preacher like my mom, and no, I never told anyone. I saw the compassion and love she had for it. She had much excitement talking about God, and when she preached, it showed all over her. I liked it when she graced the pulpit or even when she wasn't behind the podium. She demanded respect, not by her words but the life she led. Now on the natural, I wanted to be a doctor, which was a short-lived cause that took too much schooling. Remember I told you I didn't like school. I like the fact of being needed or helping someone, aiding in cures, and knowing I would make a difference.

Another fond memory from elementary school was if I didn't feel like doing my work, I would let my teacher know. When we had Parent-Teacher night, she would tell my mom that she knew when I wasn't feeling it because I would let her know. On the flip side, she told my mom I would breeze right through the lessons when I did.

I didn't go to prom and all that because I wasn't really feeling it and, I wasn't asked anyway. I didn't want to burden my mom with anything that cost extra money because she wasn't making a lot at the time, and I didn't want to add to it. Who was my childhood hero? My mom was all that I needed. She made sure I had a great childhood and tried to give me all she could. Adolescent years was grand in my book.

CHAPTER 3

SEEKING TO FIND MYSELF

In continuing my life journey, I still had it based on Proverbs 22:6. Well, now that I am older and entering the High School world to prepare for my entry into the real world, I was still trying to figure out what my purpose was in life and where I fit in. Yes, you would think with all the training and spiritual covering I had would have been enough, but it wasn't. I was still searching for validation and a sense of belonging.

I lived a sheltered life, so a lot of things I didn't understand. I didn't know how to adapt to certain things in life, but we will discuss that later. I attended North Johnston High School in Kenly, NC. It was a mixed school as well, contrary, some believed differently. I took driver's Education in my sophomore year, if memory serves me right. I took basic courses here as well. I didn't play any sports. You see, in the church I came up in, they didn't believe in women wearing pants, jewelry, makeup, going to movies, etc., so I didn't do sports or anything that went against the church policy.

So yes, I was Plain Jane. At that time, I was talking to this one guy, and no, I was not a player. I took chorus all four years while in high school. I wanted to date or talk to a guy that was respectful and loved me for me. Of course, the guys didn't even look at me, or if so, it wasn't suitable for the right reason. I did not go to my prom because I wasn't asked. Plus, I had no interest anyway. As I look back now, I was so engaged. I felt it was my Christian walk with God. I tried to watch how I carried myself. At the same time, I still felt the need to be validated for some reason. I never went to clubs and had no knowledge of the club environment until later, in my older years, and let me tell you that wasn't for me. It wasn't my life. I only had one friend that accepted me for who I was.

My first job was at Hardee's in Selma. I started as a cashier and worked my way up as Shift Manager. It didn't pay much, but for me, just starting, I felt it was a lot. I loved my job. I loved the opportunity to interact with people. I had this job through the latter part of High School. I finally graduated High School, and now world here I come. Lol. But boy, I wasn't sure I was ready for the world. So, after High School, I entered the military. I did my basic training at Fort Jackson, SC, and my AIT in Fort Lee, VA. Now it's about to get real, lol, lol, lol.

CHAPTER 4

THE HAND OF GOD IS
ALWAYS UPON ME

There is a song that says, "Down Through the Years the Lord's Been Good to Me." I did not tell my family at first that I was going into the military. During my adolescence and up to my adulthood years, I felt I had no identity. I wanted to experience LIFE. My family always encouraged us to do our best. I can do anything I set my mind to. I went in the service initially to get away from home, not that home was bad, but I guess to experiment or see how real life was. I wanted to see the world.

I enjoyed the military life. It showed me discipline. Before it was always church, church, church and I wanted to get out and live. Now I still had a job to come back to. I still had responsibilities like car payments, insurance, etc. This was actually my first time away from home, so yes, I was nervous and scared. I had the opportunity to go overseas. Let me say before I went off, my mom and grandma prayed for me and told me to act like I had some home training, which I did; besides, I was leaving home, not the presence of God.

As I traveled on, the saying is true. You never know who knows who. I got stationed in Ramstein, Germany, with my unit. Once I got all settled in, of course, I wanted to find a nice church to attend while being there. See, I told you I couldn't get away from church. And yes, I had plenty of opportunities to go partying and clubbing, and no one back home would not have known. But I would know, and God would know, and honestly, even though I was trying to find me, that wasn't where I wanted to be found.

I found this church called Greater Evangel Temple and I attended a service and afterwards mingled with the Pastor and his wife and several of the members there. There was this associate minister, Pastor Donald Altman. We talked and he started asking me where I was from and who my folks were. He asked because he saw my last name on my uniform. After we had talked for a few minutes, I learned he was from where I was born, Smithfield, NC. He knew my family very well, and I knew his somewhat. When he came stateside to visit his mom and family, he had reached out to some of my family and told them that he had met me and that I was a joy and a pleasant young lady. He told them that I had joined the church there and was a blessing by how I carried myself. It made me feel good because I could have lived any kind of way. I wanted to exemplify Christ.

Of course, when my mom got this news, she was proud and proud of me. My mom kept me encouraged when I was homesick and just wanted to come home. I would call her when I got the chance. She would cheer me up and sing this little song, 'Never Alone.' She was my Rock. I never got married and had children. When I tell people, they look at me like something is wrong with me. I must admit I love kids but have none of my own.

After I graduated from Basic Training, which I graduated on crutches (and that was the favor of God because I was supposed to be recycled). During this time, I came home and continued to work at Eaton. While in the military, I matured. I traveled to different countries and saw a lot of things. I realized the hand of God was always upon me. Even through a couple of things that happened to me in the military, which I will discuss in my next book, God has been good to me.

Later, I attended Johnston Community College when I came home from the military. I initially studied Criminal Justice. I did not graduate because I was still undecided on what I wanted my degree to be. I also went for a short while to ECPI and took up Medical Coding. God always knows how to place other things in your life to accomplish and show you your true calling.

CHAPTER 5

BEING A PK (PREACHER'S KID)

I have heard all through life through other preachers' kids that it's hard being a preacher's kid. Well, I can agree and disagree with that. When my mom would have to preach, or the choir had to sing in my adolescences, of course, I would have to go, and there were no if's, and's or but's about it. As a preacher's kid, you are held to a higher level or standard. You are viewed differently. As I grew up in my adult life in Christ, I had more of a passion for church. I always liked church because I grew up in holiness. A lot of things that other kids do we wasn't allowed to do. As I mentioned like clubs, I had never gone inside a club until five years ago. I had gone with a friend, and I see why I never went inside one; that life wasn't for me. So prior, when preachers would say, "you know how yawl was in the club, I could honestly say I couldn't relate.

On Sundays, we would get up and go to church and may not get back till that night. If we did come home, we would take our clothes off just to put them back on within two to three hours. Mom would make food for us. We would eat, and back to church we go. This went on into my earlier adolescent years. If I went somewhere Saturday night, she would tell me if you go out and come in late, you were still going to church.

So yes, in my adult life, even though I knew I didn't have to go to church as much as I did growing up, it was in me. I wanted to go. There was something at church I thirsted for. I didn't feel right not going, especially on Sunday morning. Yes, some were jealous of me because I wasn't, how do you say it? rowdy and out there. I had a lot of influential people who helped me travel this Christian walk, while yet still trying to see where I fit in and what my purpose was. I would see how my mom and grandma and other relatives would walk in their calling and be happy and all, but I was yet to understand through all the years where my purpose was.

When I came back from the military, I still attended Selma Church of God of Prophecy. Then I visited other fellowships, but when my mom became Pastor in Wilson, NC, I went there to help. I became choir director and played the piano a bit. While doing that, I became a member of The JW and the Higher Praise Mass choir, which we traveled a lot, and I loved that. I felt like I finally belonged somewhere.

As years went on, I supported my mom in Wilson, NC. In 2012 when my mom passed, I sought God for a church that taught the word like my mom would preach/teach, someone who was in depth in the word like my mom. After a couple of years, I was drawn to Harvest Word Ministry in Zebulon, NC, under the leadership of Apostle Hattie and Pastor Larry Stancil. Under this ministry, I have learned so much and have a closer walk with God. I currently sing on the praise and worship team and lead the congregation into praise and worship. This ministry has a school established that God has put in her heart. This school is called Safe Haven Interdenominational Bible College and Training Institute.

I am proud yet humbled to say I have obtained a master's degree in Biblical Studies. I'm currently attending class for my Master's in Pastoral Leadership.

I'm on the woman's ministry coordination team at Harvest Word Ministries. I'm also a member of The Women of Triumph Ministries Intl Inc., under the leadership of CEO Pastor Anna Lyons. In this ministry, I serve as the Bereavement/Birthday coordinator. In this position, I call the members when they have a birthday or in the case of a death. I call to offer comfort and encouraging words. By doing this role, it makes me feel wanted and needed. I am also the songstress for this ministry. I got involved with this ministry through Minister Diane Pace, my sister in Christ. She's the membership coordinator. This ministry has blessed me because it allows me to use my gift freely and allows me to meet other women in the faith.

CHAPTER 6

VALIDATED BY GOD

There is a song I used to sing in the choir named "If He Has to Reach Way Down Jesus Will Pick You Up." My trials and tribulations were vulnerability and getting attached to the wrong people. I told you in a previous chapter that I wanted to be validated by people. I wanted to belong and be liked. I had relationships/friendships only to find out they wanted to use me and drain my anointing. I know the bible says, "He that finds," and I'll stop there.

I was involved with a couple of people who I thought would be my mate because he was in the church. We would talk about the Bible and pray together. I just knew this could be it until one evening, as we were ending the evening, the mask came off. He only wanted sex, which was the issue with each guy I was with. It was one rejection after the other. Then there were friendships I thought were good until they really showed me who and what they were about. They didn't care about me but just wanted what they could get out of me and have control.

The rejection and validation became the story of my life for a while, but I hid it because I was a preacher's kid, and I am supposed to keep it all together. In four years, I lost almost all my immediate family one after another. I mean all the prominent people who helped shape me into who I am today. The worst blow was when I lost my best friend, my Pastor, my mom. She was all we had left, and if that wasn't enough, it was two days before my birthday. At that time, I was living in Clayton, NC. We gave her a beautiful homegoing, my siblings and me. We had a horse-drawn carriage for her. My life has not been the same since.

It was time to start the healing process, and boy, how does one heal from that? I moved back to the home house in Middlesex, NC. I think I'm still healing. I guess one reason is because I didn't know she had cancer until a few days before her death. If she knew, she didn't want me to worry. For years after her passing, I was still angry at her but I had to learn to let go.

I healed by quoting the scripture 2 Corinthians 5:9 "To be absent from the body is to be present with the Lord," and I know she was with him because she served God faithfully. Another way I heal is I think on the legacy and what she instilled in me. I continued to go to church. When I'm faced with any trials or tribulations, I remember the story of Paul when he talks about Euroclydon in Acts 27:14. He expressed it as stormy wind. So that's how I see it knowing the storm will pass over soon if I just trust the hand of God.

My family would also tell us about people being jealous of me. I couldn't imagine why. I wasn't married, I had no kids, I had my own car, home and job and was doing ok. I was told it was because of the anointing over my life. I try to remain focused on what God has for me. I try to live out the scripture in Psalm 23:5. 'He prepares a table before me in the presence of my enemies.

Like in the Bible, when God taught the disciples in parables to teach life lessons, so he taught me faith, perseverance, and integrity. No matter what life gives you and no matter how many times man may reject you, know that God says, "I still and always will love you." He tells me he will never leave me nor forsake me. He taught me that once I get delivered from ME and let him truly guide and lead me that I didn't have to be validated by people. I'm validated through his eyes. That is all I need. My mom and my sister would always stay to themselves, and I often wondered why. But now I know why. My mom taught me faith, how to live holy, and to put God first. My grandmas taught me humbleness and the value of prayer. My desire is to live a peaceful and happy life.

CHAPTER 7

I AM FEARFULLY AND WONDERFULLY MADE

All through life, I can say God has always walked with me. He said in the word, I will never leave you nor forsake you. Through my walk throughout life, I've sometimes felt the need to be validated. I've been like others lied on, mistreated, misunderstood, and rejected by those I thought were my friends. Yes, there were times when I tried to fit in. I was naive and vulnerable to a lot of things.

As I began to unmask and get delivered from me and my way of thinking and reasoning and started placing the real Unetta in God's hand and care, nothing else mattered. God showed me that I was created for his purpose. I began to quote Psalm 139:14 "I praise you because I am fearfully and wonderfully made." Once I got that fully embedded in my spirit, being validated or fitting in was no longer a feeling or thought. I began to let flesh and emotions die. I began to allow the spirit to detox me.

At the present time, I'm learning to let the Holy Spirit lead me. I attend a phenomenal church, Harvest Word Ministries, where I am the praise team leader/ exhortator. If you're reading this book, I am a first-time solo author. On Sundays I am head of the host\hostess at Abba Worship Center in Raleigh NC. I am the soloist for the Women of Triumph and the Bereavement\birthday coordinator. I'm currently looking forward to graduating with my master's degree and my plans after are to obtain my Doctoral and prayerfully write more best-selling books.

ABOUT THE AUTHOR

Unetta is a country girl born in the South Smithfield, NC but raised in Middlesex, NC. Her mother was the late Pastor Shelley Lofton. She has one sister Vernecia Lofton and one brother Dr. Antwan Lofton.

Unetta currently serve as the Bereavement \Birthday Coordinator for Women of Triumph Ministries Intl Inc. (WOT). She is also a vocalist. and can be seen singing with the JW and Higher Praise Mass Choir of Selma, NC.

She graduated from North Johnston High School in Kenly, NC. Unetta served nine years in the United States Army. Her proudest accomplishments include her graduating with honors as class Salutatorian and receiving her bachelor's degree and graduating as the class Valedictorian with her master's degree in Biblical Studies from Safe Haven Interdenominational Bible College and Training Institute.

His Glory Creations Publishing, LLC is an International Christian Book Publishing Company, which helps launch the creative fiction and non-fiction works of new, aspiring and seasoned authors across the globe, through stories that are inspirational, empowering, life-changing or educational in nature, including poetry, journals, children's books, and recipe books.

DESIRE TO KNOW MORE?

Contact Information:

CEO and Founder: Felicia C. Lucas

www.hisglorycreationspublishing.com

Email: hgcpublishingllc@gmail.com

Facebook: His Glory Creations Publishing (HGCPAC)

Instagram: Coach Felicia Lucas

Phone: 919-679-1706

www.ingramcontent.com/pod-product-compliance
Lightning Source LLC
LaVergne TN
LVHW041210080426
835508LV00008B/880